Temple Grandin
and Livestock Handling

By Virginia Loh-Hagan

21st Century
Junior Library

CHERRY LAKE
Publishing

Published in the United States of America by
Cherry Lake Publishing
Ann Arbor, Michigan
www.cherrylakepublishing.com

Content Adviser: Kirsten Edwards, MA, Educational Studies
Reading Adviser: Marla Conn, MS, Ed., Literacy specialist, Read-Ability, Inc.

Photo Credits: © pook_jun/Shutterstock.com, Cover, 1; © sirtravelalot/Shutterstock.com, 4; © Kathy Hutchins/Shutterstock.com, 6; © alanisko/Shutterstock.com, 8; © Steven Frame/Shutterstock.com, 10; © Cineberg/Shutterstock.com, 12; © Austin Community College/flickr.com, 14, 16; © Counse/flickr.com, 18; © Monkey Business Images/Shutterstock.com, 20

Copyright © 2019 by Cherry Lake Publishing
All rights reserved. No part of this book may be reproduced or utilized in any form or by any means without written permission from the publisher.

Library of Congress Cataloging-in-Publication Data
Names: Loh-Hagan, Virginia, author. | Loh-Hagan, Virginia. Women innovators.
Title: Temple Grandin and livestock handling / by Virginia Loh-Hagan.
Description: Ann Arbor [Mich.] : Cherry Lake Publishing, 2018. | Series: Women innovators |
    Includes bibliographical references and index.
Identifiers: LCCN 2018003305 | ISBN 9781534129146 (hardcover) | ISBN 9781534130845 (pdf) |
    ISBN 9781534132344 (pbk.) | ISBN 9781534134041 (hosted ebook)
Subjects: LCSH: Grandin, Temple—Juvenile literature. | Animal industry—Juvenile literature. |
    Animal specialists—Biography—Juvenile literature.
Classification: LCC SF33.G67 L64 2018 | DDC 636.0092—dc23
LC record available at https://lccn.loc.gov/2018003305

Cherry Lake Publishing would like to acknowledge the work of The Partnership for 21st Century Skills.
Please visit *www.p21.org* for more information.

Printed in the United States of America
Corporate Graphics

CONTENTS

5   A Woman

11   An Idea

17   A Legacy

22   Glossary
23   Find Out More
24   Index
24   About the Author

Livestock can include cows, pigs, horses, and chickens.

A Woman

Do you ever think about where your meat comes from? It most likely comes from livestock. Livestock are farm animals. These animals are raised for a purpose. They're either sold for food or raised to do work.

Many people don't like the way livestock are treated. Mary Temple Grandin is one of them. She is a professor of animal science and an expert on animal behavior.

Grandin worked with many educational coaches.

Grandin was born on August 29, 1947, in Boston, Massachusetts. She didn't talk until she was 4 years old. Doctors said she had brain damage. But she later found out she has **autism**. Her mother made sure Grandin got the best care.

Grandin has a hard time interacting with other people. As a child, she was teased

Think!

Think about ways that you're different from others. Are you teased because of your differences? How does that make you feel?

Grandin likes working with cows best.

for having **tics** and for being different. Growing up was tough for her.

She spent a summer at a farm in Arizona when she was 15. This changed her life. She learned that she had a lot in common with animals. She sees the world in pictures, not words. She believes this is how animals see the world as well.

Grandin earned a **doctorate** in animal science. She writes books and gives speeches. She teaches farms how to improve animals' lives.

Before Grandin, animal handlers used whips and prods.

10

An Idea

As a person with autism, Grandin experiences daily struggles. She is very **sensitive** to noise and change. Animals are sensitive, too. Because of this, she says she can relate to animals.

She designed more **humane** ways to handle animals raised for food. She does not support the use of force. She encourages **handlers** to reduce fear and

Bruised meat caused by unkind
handling can't be sold.

stress in animals. Scared animals are at risk of getting hurt.

Livestock raised for food need to be moved into meat processing buildings. Handlers normally move livestock in ways that are easier for people, not animals. Grandin changed this.

She invented **diagonal** pens. It was more natural to the animals. It also kept animals from hanging out in corners or the middle of the pen. Animals naturally moved toward the loading **chutes**.

She invented curved loading chutes. First, livestock are shielded from seeing what's ahead. This keeps them calm.

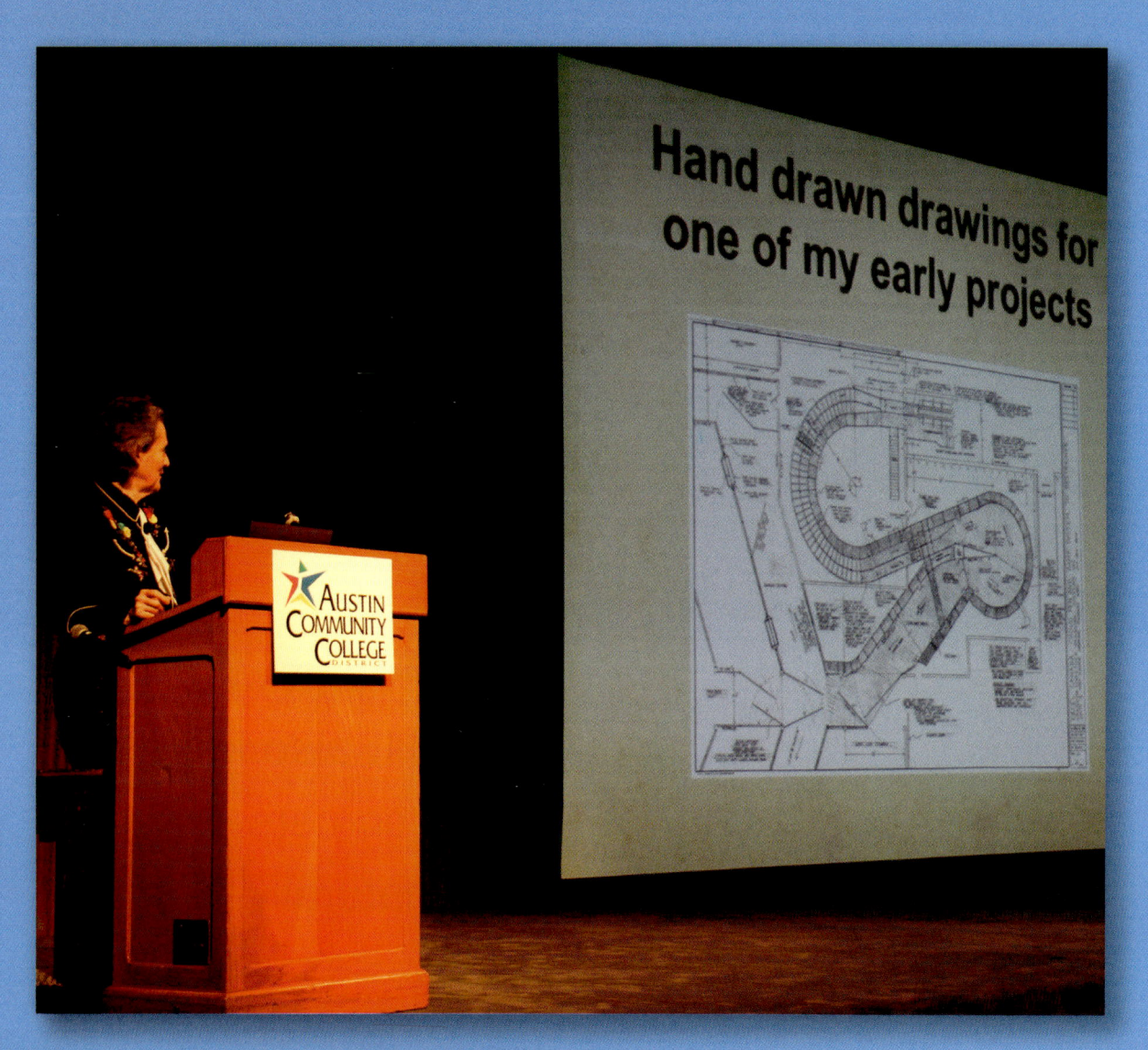

Curved chutes use animals' herding instincts.

Second, the curved shape makes animals think they're circling back to where they started.

Grandin invented a safe system for animals that enter a meat processing building. Animals are held in place with straps that hug their chests and stomachs. They ride a **conveyor belt**. This makes them more comfortable.

Ask Questions!

Talk to someone who works with animals. Ask questions about animals. Learn more about the way they behave. Learn more about ways you can help them.

Grandin created a rating system to measure animal handling.

A Legacy

Grandin is the voice for those without one. Her **legacy** can be seen on livestock farms. Her inventions are used everywhere. She changed the way farmers treat animals. She devotes her life to making animals feel safe. She said, "Animals are not things."

Her work with autism is also part of her legacy. She has done a lot to educate people on autism. She encourages the idea

Grandin speaks a lot about autism.

that being different is not being less of a person.

Grandin often combines her knowledge about animals and autism. One of her most popular inventions is the "hug box."

She invented the hug box when she was 18. She saw handlers lead animals into a tight space to get shots of medicine. Gentle pressure was applied to calm the animals. Grandin adapted this idea. She made a **device** that applies pressure to help calm people. Her hug box has helped many people with autism.

Grandin has earned many awards for her work. She was honored by the American

Grandin's books are taught in college classes.

Academy of Arts and Sciences. She was also honored in the National Women's Hall of Fame. She has appeared on many television and radio shows. There's even a movie about her life.

Grandin has changed the way people think about animals. She has changed the way people think about autism.

Look!

Look around you. See how animals are treated. Go to a farm. Go to a zoo. Go to a dog park.

GLOSSARY

autism (AW-tiz-uhm) a condition that causes someone to have trouble learning, communicating, and forming relationships with people

chutes (SHOOTS) sloping channels or slides for bringing things to a lower level

conveyor belt (kuhn-VAY-ur BELT) a continuous moving band of fabric, rubber, or metal that moves objects or animals from one place to another

device (dih-VISE) a thing made or adapted for a particular purpose

diagonal (dye-AG-uh-nuhl) joining opposite corners of a square or rectangle

doctorate (DOK-ter-it) the highest degree awarded by a university

handlers (HAND-lerz) people who train or are in charge of an animal

humane (hyoo-MAYN) being kind or gentle

legacy (LEG-uh-see) something handed down from one generation to another

sensitive (SEN-sih-tiv) easily offended or upset

tics (TIKS) features of a person's behavior that are perceived to be abnormal

FIND OUT MORE

BOOKS

Barghoorn, Linda. *Temple Grandin: Pioneer for Animal Rights and Autism Awareness*. New York: Crabtree Publishing, 2017.

Mosca, Julia Finley. *The Girl Who Thought in Pictures: The Story of Dr. Temple Grandin*. Seattle: The Innovation Press, 2017.

Sepahban, Lois. *Temple Grandin: Inspiring Animal-Behavior Scientist*. Minneapolis: Core Library, 2015.

WEBSITES

Biography—Temple Grandin
https://www.biography.com/people/temple-grandin-38062
Read more about Grandin's life.

TED Talks—Temple Grandin: The World Needs All Kinds of Minds
https://www.ted.com/talks/temple_grandin_the_world_needs_all_kinds_of_minds
Watch Grandin as she talks about how her mind works.

INDEX

A
animal science, 5, 9
autism, 7, 9, 11, 17–19, 21

D
diagonal pens, 13–15

G
Grandin, Mary Temple
and autism, 7, 9, 11, 17–19, 21
awards, 19, 21
ideas about handling animals, 9, 11–16
invents hug box, 19
invents safe ways to move livestock, 13–15
legacy, 17–21
who she is, 5–9

H
hug box, 19

L
livestock, 4, 5, 13, 17
loading chutes, 13–15

M
meat, 5, 12, 13

N
National Academy of Arts and Sciences, 21
National Women's Hall of Fame, 21

ABOUT THE AUTHOR

Dr. Virginia Loh-Hagan is an author, university professor, former classroom teacher, and curriculum designer. She handles animals every day. (Her animals don't listen to her.) She lives in San Diego with her very tall husband and very naughty dogs. To learn more about her, visit www.virginialoh.com.